INSTRUCTION CONCERNING WORSHIP of the EUCHARISTIC MYSTERY

Inaestimabile Donum

Prepared by the Sacred Congregation for the
Sacraments and Divine Worship

Approved and Confirmed by His Holiness

POPE JOHN PAUL II

April 17, 1980

ST. PAUL BOOKS & MEDIA

Reprinted with permission from *L'Osservatore Romano*, English Edition.

Printed in the U.S.A., by the Daughters of St. Paul
50 St. Paul's Ave., Boston, MA 02130

St. Paul Books & Media is the publishing house of the Daughters of St. Paul, an international congregation of women religious serving the Church with the communications media.

4 5 6 7 8 9   99 98 97 96 95 94

Foreword

Following the letter that Pope John Paul II addressed on February 24, 1980, to the bishops and, through them, to the priests, and in which he again considered the priceless gift of the Holy Eucharist, the Sacred Congregation for the Sacraments and Divine Worship is calling to the bishops' attention certain norms concerning worship of this great mystery.

These indications are not a summary of everything already stated by the Holy See in the documents concerning the Eucharist promulgated since the Second Vatican Council and still in force, particularly in the *Missale Romanum*,[1] the Ritual *De Sacra Communione et de Cultu Mysterii Eucharistici Extra Missam*,[2] and the Instructions *Eucharisticum Mysterium*,[3] *Memoriale Domini*,[4] *Immensae caritatis*,[5] and *Liturgicae instaurationes*.[6]

This Sacred Congregation notes with great joy the many positive results of the liturgical reform: a more active and conscious participation by the faithful in the liturgical mysteries, doctrinal and catechetical enrichment through the use of the vernacular, and the wealth of readings from the Bible, a growth in the community sense of liturgical life, and successful efforts to close the gap between life and worship, between Liturgical piety and personal piety, and between Liturgy and popular piety.

But these encouraging and positive aspects cannot suppress concern at the varied and frequent abuses being reported from different parts of the Catholic world: the confusion of roles, especially regarding the priestly ministry and the role of the laity (indiscriminate shared recitation of the Eucharistic Prayer, homilies given by lay people, lay people distributing Communion while the priests refrain from doing so); an increasing loss of the sense of the sacred (abandonment of liturgical vestments, the Eucharist celebrated outside church without real need, lack of reverence and respect for the Blessed Sacrament, etc.); misunderstanding of the ecclesial character of the Liturgy (the use of private texts, the proliferation of unapproved Eucharistic Prayers, the manipulation of the liturgical texts for social and political ends). In these cases we are face to face with a real falsification of the Catholic Liturgy: "One who offers worship to God on the Church's behalf in a way contrary to that which is laid down by the Church with God-given authority and which is customary in the Church is guilty of falsification."[7]

None of these things can bring good results. The consequences are—and cannot fail to be—the impairing of the unity of Faith and worship in the Church, doctrinal uncertainty, scandal and bewilderment among the People of God, and the near inevitability of violent reactions.

The faithful have a right to a true Liturgy, which means the Liturgy desired and laid down by the Church, which has in fact indicated where adaptations may be made as called for by pastoral requirements in different places or by different groups of people. Undue experimentation, changes and creativity bewilder the faithful. The use of unauthorized texts means a loss of the necessary connection between the *lex orandi* and the *lex credendi*. The Second Vatican Council's admonition in this regard must be remembered: "No person, even if he be a priest, may add, remove or change anything in the Liturgy on his own authority."[8] And Paul VI of venerable memory stated that: "Anyone who takes advantage of the reform to indulge in arbitrary experiments is wasting energy and offending the ecclesial sense."[9]

a) The Mass

1. "The two parts which in a sense go to make up the Mass, namely the Liturgy of the Word and the Eucharistic Liturgy, are so closely connected that they form but one single act of worship."[10] A person should not approach the table of the Bread of the Lord without having first been at the table of His Word.[11] Sacred Scripture is therefore of the highest importance in the celebration of Mass. Consequently there can be no disregarding what the Church has laid down in order to insure that "in sacred celebrations there should be a more ample, more varied and more suitable reading from Sacred Scripture."[12] The norms laid down in the Lectionary concerning the number of readings, and the directives given for special occasions are to be observed. It would be a serious abuse to replace the Word of God with the word of man, no matter who the author may be.[13]

2. The reading of the Gospel passage is reserved to the ordained minister, namely the deacon or the priest. When possible, the other readings should be entrusted to a reader who has been instituted as such, or to other spiritually and technically trained lay people. The first reading is followed by a responsorial psalm, which is an integral part of the Liturgy of the Word.[14]

3. The purpose of the homily is to explain to the faithful the Word of God proclaimed in the readings, and to apply its message to the present. Accordingly the homily is to be given by the priest or the deacon.[15]

4. It is reserved to the priest, by virtue of his ordination, to proclaim the Eucharistic Prayer, which of its nature is the high point of the whole celebration. It is therefore an abuse to have some parts of the Eucharistic Prayer said by the deacon, by a lower minister, or by the faithful.[16] On the other hand the assembly does not remain passive and inert; it unites itself to the priest in faith and silence and shows its concurrence by the various interventions provided for in the course of the Eucharistic Prayer: the responses to the Preface dialogue, the *Sanctus*, the acclamation after the Consecration, and the final *Amen* after the *Per Ipsum*. The *Per Ipsum* itself is reserved to the priest. This *Amen* especially should be emphasized by being sung, since it is the most important in the whole Mass.

5. Only the Eucharistic Prayers included in the Roman Missal or those that the Apostolic See has by law admitted, in the manner and within the limits laid down by the Holy See, are to be used. To modify the Eucharistic Prayers approved by the Church or to adopt others privately composed is a most serious abuse.

6. It should be remembered that the Eucharistic Prayer must not be overlaid with other prayers or songs.[17] When proclaiming the Eucharistic Prayer, the priest is to pronounce the text clearly, so as to make it easy for the faithful to understand it, and so as to foster the formation of a true assembly entirely intent upon the celebration of the memorial of the Lord.

7. *Concelebration*, which has been restored in the Western Liturgy, manifests in an exceptional manner the

unity of the priesthood. Concelebrants must, therefore, pay careful attention to the signs that indicate that unity. For example, they are to be present from the beginning of the celebration, they are to wear the prescribed vestments, they are to occupy the place appropriate to their ministry as concelebrants, and they are to observe faithfully the other norms for the seemly performance of the rite.[18]

8. *Matter of the Eucharist.* Faithful to Christ's example, the Church has constantly used bread and wine mixed with water to celebrate the Lord's Supper. The bread for the celebration of the Eucharist, in accordance with the tradition of the whole Church, must be made solely of wheat, and, in accordance with the tradition proper to the Latin Church, it must be unleavened. By reason of the sign, the matter of the Eucharistic celebration "should appear as actual food." This is to be understood as linked to the consistency of the bread, and not to its form, which remains the traditional one. No other ingredients are to be added to the wheaten flour and water. The preparation of the bread requires attentive care to ensure that the product does not detract from the dignity due to the Eucharistic bread, can be broken in a dignified way, does not give rise to excessive fragments, and does not offend the sensibilities of the faithful when they eat it. The wine for the Eucharistic celebration must be of "the fruit of the vine" (Lk. 22:18) and be natural and genuine, that is to say not mixed with other substances.[19]

9. *Eucharistic Communion.* Communion is a gift of the Lord, given to the faithful through the minister appointed for this purpose. It is not permitted that the

faithful should themselves pick up the consecrated bread and the sacred chalice, still less that they should hand them from one to another.

10. The faithful, whether religious or lay, who are authorized as extraordinary ministers of the Eucharist can distribute Communion only when there is no priest, deacon or acolyte, when the priest is impeded by illness or advanced age, or when the number of the faithful going to Communion is so large as to make the celebration of Mass excessively long.[20] Accordingly, a reprehensible attitude is shown by those priests who, though present at the celebration, refrain from distributing Communion and leave this task to the laity.

11. The Church has always required from the faithful respect and reverence for the Eucharist at the moment of receiving it.

With regard to the manner of going to Communion, the faithful can receive it either kneeling or standing, in accordance with the norms laid down by the episcopal conference: "When the faithful communicate kneeling, no other sign of reverence towards the Blessed Sacrament is required, since kneeling is itself a sign of adoration. When they receive Communion standing, it is strongly recommended that, coming up in procession, they should make a sign of reverence before receiving the Sacrament. This should be done at the right time and place, so that the order of people going to and from Communion is not disrupted."[21]

The *Amen* said by the faithful when receiving Communion is an act of personal faith in the presence of Christ.

12. With regard to Communion under both kinds, the norms laid down by the Church must be observed,

both by reason of the reverence due to the Sacrament and for the good of those receiving the Eucharist, in accordance with variations in circumstances, times and places.[22]

Episcopal conferences and ordinaries also are not to go beyond what is laid down in the present discipline: the granting of permission for Communion under both kinds is not to be indiscriminate, and the celebrations in question are to be specified precisely; the groups that use this faculty are to be clearly defined, well disciplined, and homogeneous.[23]

13. Even after Communion the Lord remains present under the species. Accordingly, when Communion has been distributed, the sacred particles remaining are to be consumed or taken by the competent minister to the place where the Eucharist is reserved.

14. On the other hand, the consecrated wine is to be consumed immediately after Communion and may not be kept. Care must be taken to consecrate only the amount of wine needed for Communion.

15. The rules laid down for the purification of the chalice and the other sacred vessels that have contained the Eucharistic species must be observed.[24]

16. Particular respect and care are due to the sacred vessels, both the chalice and paten for the celebration of the Eucharist, and the ciboria for the Communion of the faithful. The form of the vessels must be appropriate for the liturgical use for which they are meant. The material must be noble, durable, and in every case adapted to sacred use. In this sphere, judgment belongs to the episcopal conference of the individual regions.

Use is not to be made of simple baskets or other recipients meant for ordinary use outside the sacred celebrations, nor are the sacred vessels to be of poor quality or lacking any artistic style.

Before being used, chalices and patens must be blessed by the bishop or by a priest.[25]

17. The faithful are to be recommended not to omit to make a proper thanksgiving after Communion. They may do this during the celebration with a period of silence, with a hymn, psalm or other song of praise,[26] or also after the celebration, if possible by staying behind to pray for a suitable time.

18. There are, of course, various roles that women can perform in the liturgical assembly: these include reading the Word of God and proclaiming the intentions of the Prayer of the Faithful. Women are not, however, permitted to act as altar servers.[27]

19. Particular vigilance and special care are recommended with regard to Masses transmitted by the audiovisual media. Given their very wide diffusion, their celebration must be of exemplary quality.[28]

In the case of celebrations that are held in private houses, the norms of the Instruction *Actio pastoralis* of May 15, 1969, are to be observed.[29]

b) Eucharistic Worship
Outside Mass

20. Public and private devotion to the Holy Eucharist outside Mass also is highly recommended: for the presence of Christ, who is adored by the faithful in the Sacrament, derives from the sacrifice and is directed towards sacramental and spiritual Communion.

21. When Eucharistic devotions are arranged, account should be taken of the liturgical season, so that they

harmonize with the Liturgy, draw inspiration from it in some way, and lead the Christian people toward it.[30]

22. With regard to exposition of the Holy Eucharist, either prolonged or brief, and with regard to processions of the Blessed Sacrament, Eucharistic Congresses, and the whole ordering of Eucharistic piety, the pastoral indications and directives given in the Roman Ritual are to be observed.[31]

23. It must not be forgotten that "before the blessing with the Sacrament, an appropriate time should be devoted to the reading of the Word of God, to songs and prayers, and to some silent prayer."[32] At the end of the adoration, a hymn is sung, and a prayer chosen from among the many contained in the Roman Ritual is recited or sung.[33]

24. The *tabernacle* in which the Eucharist is kept can be located on an altar, or away from it, in a spot in the church which is very prominent, truly noble, and duly decorated, or in a chapel suitable for private prayer and for adoration by the faithful.[34]

25. The tabernacle should be solid, unbreakable, and not transparent.[35] The presence of the Eucharist is to be indicated by a tabernacle veil or by some other suitable means laid down by the competent authority, and a lamp must perpetually burn before it, as a sign of honor paid to the Lord.[36]

26. The venerable practice of genuflecting before the Blessed Sacrament, whether enclosed in the tabernacle or publicly exposed, as a sign of adoration, is to be maintained.[37] This act requires that it be performed in a recollected way. In order that the heart may bow before God in profound reverence, the genuflection must be neither hurried nor careless.

27. If anything has been introduced that is at variance with these indications, it is to be corrected.

Most of the difficulties encountered in putting into practice the reform of the Liturgy and especially the reform of the Mass stem from the fact that neither priests nor faithful have perhaps been sufficiently aware of the theological and spiritual reasons for which the changes have been made, in accordance with the principles laid down by the Council.

Priests must acquire an ever deeper understanding of the authentic way of looking at the Church,[38] of which the celebration of the Liturgy and especially of the Mass is the living expression. Without an adequate biblical training, priests will not be able to present to the faithful the meaning of the Liturgy as an enactment, in signs, of the history of salvation. Knowledge of the history of the Liturgy will likewise contribute to an understanding of the changes which have been introduced, and introduced not for the sake of novelty but as a revival and adaptation of authentic and genuine tradition.

The Liturgy also requires great balance, for, as the Constitution *Sacrosanctum concilium* says, it "is thus the outstanding means by which the faithful can express in their lives, and manifest to others, the mystery of Christ and the real nature of the true Church. It is of the essence of the Church that she be both human and divine, visible and yet invisibly endowed, eager to act and yet devoted to contemplation, present in this world and yet not at home in it. She is all these things in such a way that in her the human is directed and subordinated to the divine, the visible likewise to the invisible, action to contemplation, and this present world to that city yet to come, which we seek."[39] Without this balance, the true face of Christian Liturgy becomes obscured.

In order to reach these ideals more easily it will be necessary to foster liturgical formation in seminaries and faculties[40] and to facilitate the participation of priests in courses, meetings, assemblies or liturgical weeks, in which study and reflection should be properly complemented by model celebrations. In this way priests will be able to devote themselves to more effective pastoral action, to liturgical catechesis of the faithful, to organizing groups of lectors, to giving altar servers spiritual and practical training, to training animators of the assembly, to enriching progressively the repertoire of songs, in a word to all the initiatives favoring an ever deeper understanding of the Liturgy.

In the implementation of the liturgical reform, great responsibility falls upon national and diocesan liturgical commissions and liturgical institutes and centers, especially in the work of translating the liturgical books and training the clergy and faithful in the spirit of the reform desired by the Council.

The work of these bodies must be at the service of the ecclesiastical authority, which should be able to count upon their faithful collaboration. Such collaboration must be faithful to the Church's norms and directives, and free of arbitrary initiatives and particular ways of acting that could compromise the fruits of the liturgical renewal.

This document will come into the hands of God's ministers in the first decade of the life of the *Missale Romanum* promulgated by Pope Paul VI following the prescriptions of the Second Vatican Council.

It seems fitting to recall a remark made by that Pope concerning fidelity to the norms governing celebration: "It is a very serious thing when division is introduced precisely where *congregavit nos in unum Christi amor,* in the Liturgy and the Eucharistic Sacrifice, by the refusing of obedience to the norms laid down in the liturgical sphere. It is in the name of tradition that we ask all our sons and daughters, all the Catholic communities, to celebrate with dignity and fervor the renewed Liturgy."[41]

The bishops, "whose function it is to control, foster, and safeguard the entire liturgical life of the Church entrusted to them,"[42] will not fail to discover the most suitable means for ensuring a careful and firm application of these norms, for the glory of God and the good of the Church.

Rome, April 3, 1980, Holy Thursday.

This instruction, prepared by the Sacred Congregation for the Sacraments and Divine Worship, was approved on April 17, 1980, by the Holy Father, John Paul II, who confirmed it with his own authority and ordered it to be published and to be observed by all concerned.

James R. Cardinal Knox
Prefect
Virgilio Noe
Assistant Secretary

Footnotes

1. Ed. Typica Altera, Rome, 1975.

2. Ed Typica, Rome, 1973.

3. Sacred Congregation of Rites, May 25, 1967: *AAS* 59 (1967), pp. 539-573.

4. Sacred Congregation for Divine Worship, May 29, 1969: *AAS* 61 (1969), pp. 541-545.

5. Sacred Congregation for the Discipline of the Sacraments, January 29, 1973: *AAS* 65 (1973), pp. 264-271.

6. Sacred Congregation for Divine Worship, September 5, 1970: *AAS* 62 (1970), pp. 692-704.

7. St. Thomas, *Summa Theologiae,* 2-2, Q. 93, A. 1.

8. Second Vatican Council, Constitution on the Sacred Liturgy, *Sacrosanctum concilium,* nos. 22, 3.

9. Paul VI, address of August 22, 1973: *L'Osservatore Romano,* August 23, 1973.

10. Second Vatican Council, Constitution on the Sacred Liturgy, *Sacrosanctum concilium,* no. 56.

11. Cf. *ibid.,* 56; cf. also Second Vatican Council, Dogmatic Constitution on Divine Revelation, *Dei Verbum,* no. 21.

12. Second Vatican Council, Constitution on the Sacred Liturgy, *Sacrosanctum concilium,* no. 35.

13. Cf. Sacred Congregation for Divine Worship, Instruction *Liturgicae instaurationes,* no. 2, a.

14. Cf. *Institutio Generalis Missalis Romani,* no. 36.

15. Cf. Sacred Congregation for Divine Worship, Instruction *Liturgicae instaurationes,* no. 2, a.

16. Cf. Sacred Congregation for Divine Worship, circular letter *Eucharistiae participationem,* April 27, 1973: *AAS* 65 (1973), pp. 340-347, 8; Instruction *Liturgicae instaurationes,* no. 4.

17. *Institutio Generalis Missalis Romani,* no. 12.

18. Cf. *ibid.,* nos. 156, 161-163.

19. Cf. *ibid.,* nos. 281-284; Sacred Congregation for Divine Worship, Instruction *Liturgicae instaurationes,* no. 5; *Notitiae* 6 (1970), no. 37.

20. Cf. Sacred Congregation for the Discipline of the Sacraments, Instruction *Immensae caritatis,* no. 1.

21. Sacred Congregation of Rites, Instruction *Eucharisticum Mysterium,* no. 34. Cf. *Institutio Generalis Missalis Romani,* nos. 244 c, 246 b, 247 b.

22. Cf. *Institutio Generalis Missalis Romani,* nos. 241-242.

23. Cf. *ibid.,* end of no. 242.

24. Cf. *ibid.,* no. 238.

25. Cf. *Institutio Generalis Missalis Romani,* nos. 288, 289, 292, 295; Sacred Congregation for Divine Worship, Instruction *Liturgicae instaurationes,* no. 8; *Pontificale Romanum, ordo dedicationis ecclesiae et altaris,* p. 125, no. 3.

26. Cf. *Institutio Generalis Missalis Romani,* no. 56 j.

27. Cf. Sacred Congregation for Divine Worship, Instruction *Liturgicae instaurationes,* no. 7.

28. Cf. Second Vatican Council, Constitution on the Sacred Liturgy, *Sacrosanctum concilium,* no. 20; Pontifical Commission for Social Communications, Instruction *Communio et progressio,* May 23, 1971: *AAS* 63 (1971), pp. 593-656, no. 151.

29. *AAS* 61 (1969), pp. 806-811.

30. Cf. *Rituale Romanum, De Sacra Communione et de Cultu Mysterii Eucharistici Extra Missam,* nos. 79-80.

31. Cf. *ibid.,* nos. 82-112.

32. *Ibid.,* no. 89.

33. Cf. *ibid.,* no. 97.

34. Cf. *Institutio Generalis Missalis Romani,* no. 276.

35. Cf. *Rituale Romanum, De Sacra Communione et de Cultu Mysterii Eucharistici Extra Missam,* no. 10.

36. Cf. Sacred Congregation of Rites, Instruction *Eucharisticum Mysterium,* no. 57.

37. Cf. *Rituale Romanum, De Sacra Communione et de Cultu Mysterii Eucharistici Extra Missam,* no. 84.

38. Cf. Second Vatican Council, Dogmatic Constitution on the Church, *Lumen gentium.*

39. Second Vatican Council, Constitution on the Sacred Liturgy, *Sacrosanctum concilium,* no. 2.

40. Cf. Sacred Congregation for Catholic Education, Instruction on liturgical formation in seminaries *In Ecclesiasticam Futurorum Sacerdotum Formationem,* June 3, 1979.

41. Consistorial address of May 24, 1976: *AAS* 68 (1976), p. 374.

42. Second Vatican Council, Decree *Christus Dominus,* no. 15.